If This Is a Lecture,
How Long Will It Be?

Other For Better or For Worse® Books

What, Me Pregnant?
For Better or For Worse: The 10th Anniversary Collection
Pushing 40
It's All Downhill From Here
Keep the Home Fries Burning
The Last Straw
Just One More Hug
It Must Be Nice to Be Little
Is This "One of Those Days," Daddy?
I've Got the One-More-Washload Blues

If This Is a Lecture, How Long Will It Be?

A For Better or For Worse® Collection by Lynn Johnston

Andrews and McMeel
A Universal Press Syndicate Company
Kansas City

For Better or For Worse® is syndicated internationally by Universal Press Syndicate.

If This Is a Lecture, How Long Will It Be? copyright © 1990 by Lynn Johnston. All rights reserved. Printed in the United States of America. No part of this book may be used or reproduced in any manner whatsoever without written permission except in the case of reprints in the context of reviews. For information, write Andrews and McMeel, a Universal Press Syndicate Company, 4900 Main Street, Kansas City, Missouri 64112.

ISBN: 0-8362-1821-3
Library of Congress Catalog Card Number: 90-82674

First Printing, August 1990
Fifth Printing, March 1992

28

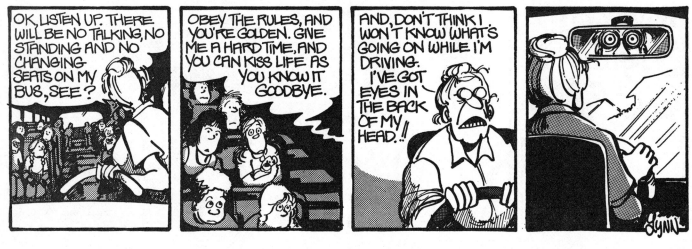

Panel 1: GET REAL, GORDO! / REDNECK HAT AN' MIRROR SHADES—THE ULTIMATE IN H.A. PROTECTION.

Panel 2: IF ALLYSON CREEMORE, OR ANY OTHER LIFE-THREATENING OBJECT, CROSSES MY LINE OF VISION, THESE WILL DEFLECT OR DIMINISH MOST OF THE HARMFUL RAYS!

Panel 3: LOOK! THERE SHE IS!! / AAAAGH!!

Panel 4: GREAT. ALL I DID WAS CHEW THE COIL OFF MY SCRIBBLER.

Panel 5: SPEAKING OF DANGEROUS OBJECTS, MIKE—HOW'S MARTHA? / I DUNNO.

Panel 6: WE'RE NOT REALLY FRIENDS ANYMORE. AFTER I TOLD HER I REALLY LIKED HER, SHE GOT BORED, I GUESS, AN' STARTED HANGING 'ROUND WITH SOMEONE ELSE.

Panel 7: BUT I DON'T CARE. WHY SHOULD I CARE? LIKE, SO WHAT, RIGHT? IT WAS NOTHING. NO BIG DEAL. WHO CARES?

Panel 8: I'M GLAD TO SEE IT DOESN'T BOTHER YOU.

44

45

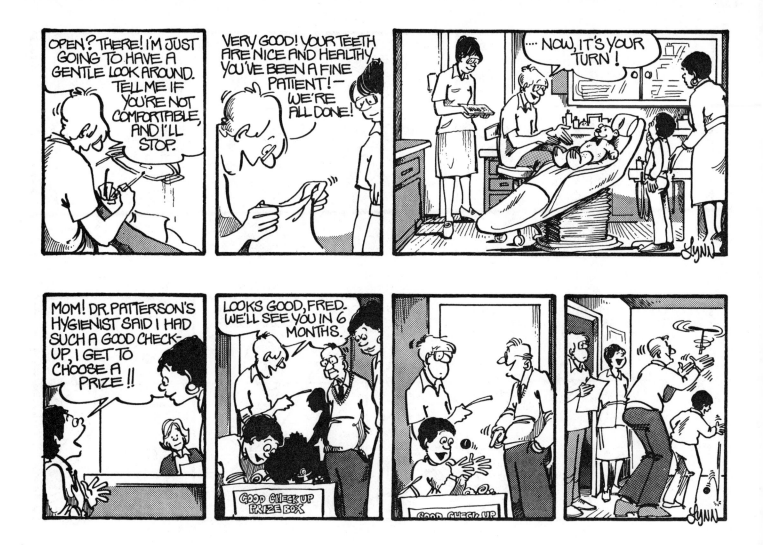

52

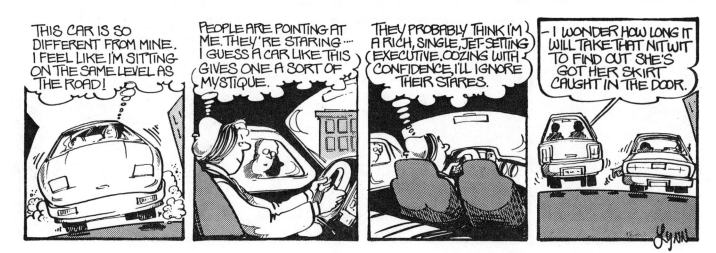

53

54

BOY, IS DAD GONNA FREAK WHEN HE COMES HOME AN' SEES WHAT YOU DID TO HIS CAR!

MICHAEL, IT WASN'T MY FAULT! THERE'S NO WAY THAT ACCIDENT COULD HAVE BEEN AVOIDED.

ANYWAY THERE'S NOTHING TO WORRY ABOUT. NO MATTER WHAT HAPPENS, YOUR FATHER IS ALWAYS EVEN TEMPERED AND RATIONAL.

I DON'T CARE IF SHE'S IN PERTH, AUSTRALIA-I WANT TO TALK TO THE MANAGER!!!

DAD'S HOME, MOM. WHEN ARE YOU GONNA TELL HIM WHAT HAPPENED TO HIS CAR?

I DON'T KNOW.

IT DEPENDS ON WHAT SORT OF MOOD HE'S IN. IF HE'S IN A GOOD MOOD, I'LL TELL HIM RIGHT NOW.

GET OUT OF MY CHAIR!!!

... TAKE YOUR TIME.

BOY, WHAT A TRIP. EVERYTHING WENT WRONG.

I HAD NO RESERVATION AT THE HOTEL, THE SPEAKER WE WENT TO HEAR NEVER SHOWED UP...

- IT WAS A MISERABLE TIME, LET ME TELL YOU.

... I MIGHT JUST AS WELL HAVE STAYED HOME.

OOH! OW! OOF! ASH!

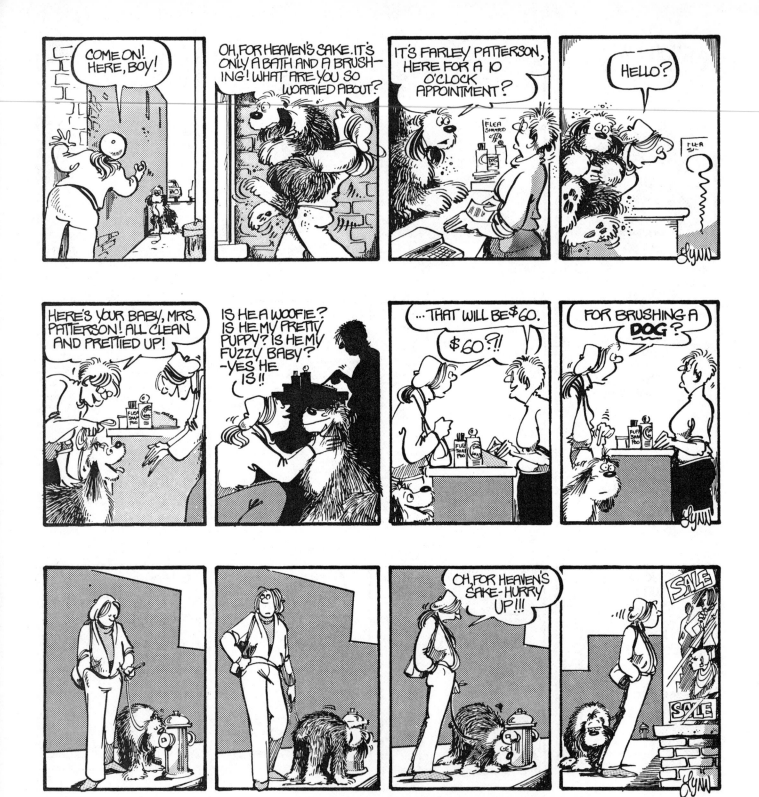

I'VE BEEN TO COURT BEFORE, EL. TRUST ME, THERE'S NOTHING TO IT.

YOU JUST GO IN THERE AND FOLLOW DIRECTIONS. THEY TELL YOU WHEN TO STAND, WHEN TO SIT, WHAT TO SAY AND WHEN TO SAY IT.

MIND YOU, I THINK IT WOULD BE HELPFUL IF YOU HAD THE BENEFIT OF SOME LEGAL COUNSEL.

COME WITH ME!!!

COURTROOM 3 ...HERE WE ARE.

PROVINCIAL TRAFFIC COURT

WHO ARE ALL THESE PEOPLE?

THEY'RE HERE FOR THE SAME REASON YOU ARE, EL—TO CONTEST A TRAFFIC TICKET.

YOU MEAN, WE ALL GET TO WATCH EACH OTHER?

A COURTROOM IS OPEN TO THE PUBLIC, EL. ANYONE CAN COME IN HERE.

I FEEL FUNNY.

I'LL ASK THE GUY IN THE BACK WHERE HE GOT HIS COFFEE.

I'VE LOOKED AROUND THE COURTROOM, CONNIE.—I DON'T THINK THE GUY WHO RAN INTO ME IS HERE.

WHAT DID HE LOOK LIKE?

LET'S SEE—GREASY, UNSHAVEN, LONG HAIR, LEATHER JACKET.... HE LOOKED LIKE A BIKER. — PROBABLY HAD A SKULL TATTOOED SOMEWHERE.

IS A MR. PERVRETT HERE?

PRESENT, SIR.

CONNIE!—THAT'S HIM!

... I THINK WE'RE IN TROUBLE, EL.

65

69

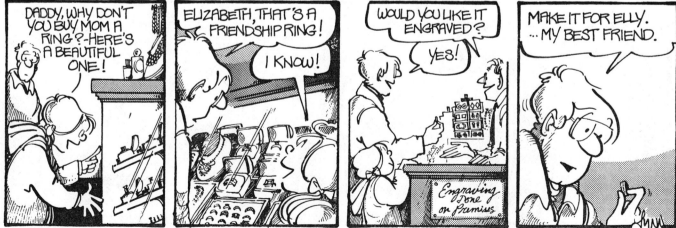

SIT DOWN, YOU TWO. IT'S ABOUT TIME YOU LEARNED SOMETHING ABOUT HOME HEATING.

DURING THE WINTER, IT COSTS US ABOUT $2,000 TO KEEP THIS HOUSE WARM. EVERY TIME YOU TURN UP THE THERMOSTAT, IT COSTS MONEY!

—I WANT YOU TO THINK ABOUT THAT BEFORE YOU GO COMPLAINING ABOUT THE TEMPERATURE IN HERE!

...HOW WARM CAN WE GET FOR A BUCK?

BRRRR... I WONDER WHAT'S WRONG—IT'S USUALLY SO WARM OVER HERE.

SHIVER SHIVER

ALSO, THERE'S A CERTAIN... SMELL.

EITHER ANNIE'S KID STUFFED SOCKS IN THE BASEBOARD HEATER AGAIN, OR...

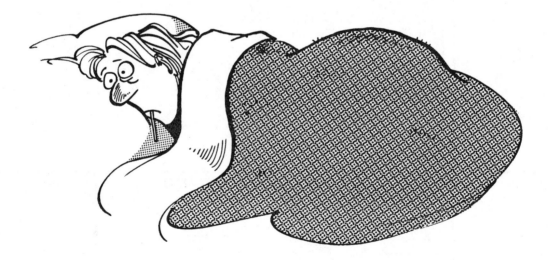

93

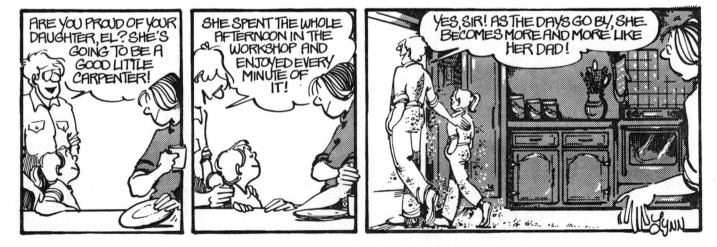

109

HI, UM, ALLYSON? IT'S, UM MIKE PATTERSON. YEAH, UM, HI!

WE, UH, I'VE GOT A FRIEND HERE-YOU KNOW GORDON? WELL WE'RE GOING TO A SHOW TONIGHT, AN' HE WANTS TO TALK TO YOU.

GO ON! UNGKK!!

TECHNICAL DIFFICULTIES ARE TEMPORARY. PLEASE DON'T ADJUST YOUR PHONE. HLGFTZ!

HI, UH, ALLYSON? IT'S ME, GORDON. I KNOW IT'S SHORT NOTICE, BUT A BUNCH OF US ARE GOING OUT TO-NIGHT, AN' I WAS WONDER-ING IF YOU'D LIKE TO....

OH, YOU ARE, HUH. NO, I UNDERSTAND. SURE! WELL, I'LL SEE YOU, YEAH. UM.....'BYE.

SHE CAN'T COME. SHE SAYS SHE HAS TO BABY-SIT. SO... HOW COME YOU'RE SMIL-ING?

... IT'S JUST NICE TO HEAR THE SOUND OF HER VOICE.

I DON'T HAVE A DATE, BUT YOU AN'MART WON'T MIND IF I TAG ALONG TONIGHT, WILL YOU? WELL, ACTUALLY...

I WON'T SIT WITH YOU OR ANYTHING.... I'LL JUST, LIKE, BLEND IN WITH THE CROWD. BUT...

HONEST, MIKE. TRUST ME! YOU WON'T EVEN KNOW I'M THERE.

Panel 1: IT'S CROWDED TONIGHT. —SEE ANYBODY YOU KNOW? YEAH!

Panel 2: THERE'S JASON, AN' MATT, AN' PETER KENT—WITH ALLYSON!

Panel 3: ALLYSON'S HERE? WITH PETER? SHE SAID SHE HAD TO BABY-SIT, MIKE! —SHE **LIED** TO ME!!

Panel 4: NOT EXACTLY, GORD. ...YOU NEVER ASKED HER THE AGE OF THE BABY!

Panel 5: WHY WOULD ALLYSON GO OUT WITH PETER WHEN HE TREATS HER SO BADLY? SHE COULD DATE ANY GUY IN SCHOOL... WHY <u>HIM</u>?

Panel 6: I'D NEVER HURT HER. SHE'D NEVER HAVE TO GUESS WITH ME. SHE'D ALWAYS KNOW WHERE I WAS AND HOW I FELT. I'D TREAT HER WITH RESPECT! —I'D CARE!!

Panel 7: WHY WOULD SHE PREFER A GUY WHO TREATS HER GREAT ONE MINUTE AND LOUSY THE NEXT? WHAT IS THERE ABOUT PETER KENT THAT'S MISSING WITH <u>ME</u>?

Panel 8: ....MAYBE IT'S THE ELEMENT OF SURPRISE.

Panel 9: LIGHTEN UP, GORD —ALLYSON ISN'T WORTH GETTING BUMMED OUT OVER. YEAH. SURE.

Panel 10: BELIEVE ME, DATING ISN'T AS GREAT AS YOU THINK IT IS. YOU'RE PROBABLY BETTER OFF NOT HAVING A GIRL-FRIEND. SNORT.

Panel 11: FOR ONE THING, IT'LL COST YOU YOUR FREEDOM —AN' THAT'S NOT ALL! WHAT DO YOU MEAN?

Panel 12: ....TONIGHT, IT COST ME EIGHTEEN DOLLARS AN' SIXTY-FIVE CENTS!

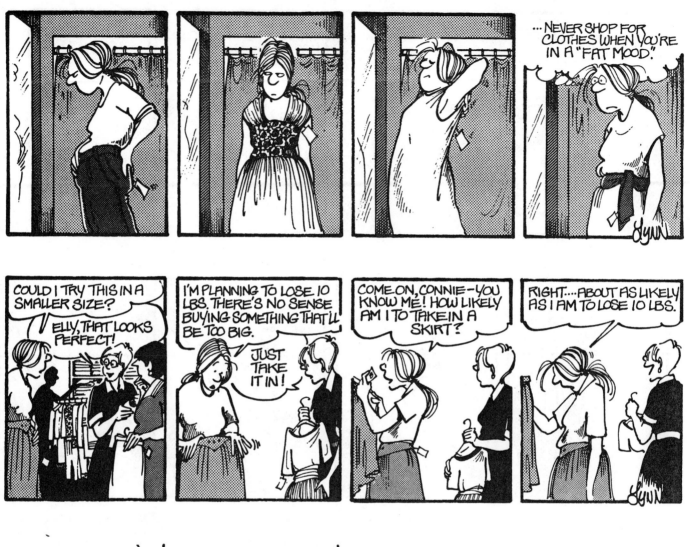

...NEVER SHOP FOR CLOTHES WHEN YOU'RE IN A "FAT MOOD."

COULD I TRY THIS IN A SMALLER SIZE?

ELLY, THAT LOOKS PERFECT!

I'M PLANNING TO LOSE 10 LBS. THERE'S NO SENSE BUYING SOMETHING THAT'LL BE TOO BIG.

JUST TAKE IT IN!

COME ON, CONNIE - YOU KNOW ME! HOW LIKELY AM I TO TAKE IN A SKIRT?

RIGHT....ABOUT AS LIKELY AS I AM TO LOSE 10 LBS.

THE CHICKEN LOOKS GOOD.

I'M CUTTING DOWN. I'LL JUST HAVE THE SALAD BAR.

WHAT ABOUT THE SOUP?

NOODLES ARE TOO FILLING. I'LL JUST HAVE THE SALAD BAR.

NO ROLL FOR ME, THANKS. I'M JUST HAVING THE SALAD BAR.